AF256143

Hello

Written by Reese Traves

Illustrated by Jon Traves

Cars honking.

Neon buzzing.

People busying.

This was the heyday of
a road called Route 66.

Ooh! Ahh!

SUNSHINE

SUNSHINE
THEATRE

2:30 7:00 8:00 ★★ NOW PLAYING ★★ 2:30 7:00 8:00

BOX OFFICE

Hotel

DIAMONDS
WATCHES
CROWN
JEWELRY

EMERALDS DIAMONDS

FLOWERS

HARDWARE

DINER DINER

SALE

BOOTS

But before it looked like this...
ELECTRICITY
PUBLIC SERVICE COMPANY of NM
Reddy Kilowatt
BANK
NATIONAL BANK
LIBERTY CAFE
KINGS HOTEL
NATIONAL BANK
FIVE + DIME
5¢ + 10¢
BARBER
COFFEE
LIBERTY CAFE
JEWELRY
SALE!
STUN HER WITH A BEAUTIFUL DIAMOND

It looked like this.

Cars bumping. Mud splashing. Tires plopping.

People got lost and stuck on old roads.

This got people talking. Minds thinking. Movements going. Two men, Cyrus Avery and John T. Woodruff wanted a new road called Route 66.

Route 66 connected main streets in big busy cities
to those in the tiniest of towns.
It starts in Chicago, Illinois
crossing 8 states for over 2,200 miles
and ends at the Santa Monica Pier.

That's a long road!

WELCOME
ADRIAN, TEXAS
ROUTE US 66
MIDPOINT
LOS ANGELES 1139 MILES
CHICAGO 1139
MIDPOINT CAFE
mmm...pie
ROUTE US 66
MIDPOINT MIDPOINT
Dell Rhea CHICKEN BASKET
HISTORIC ILLINOIS US 66 ROUTE BEGIN
LAKE MICHIGAN
ILLINOIS
Chicago
Wilmington
Livingston
Collinsville
St. Louis
MISSOURI
Springfield
Galena
KANSAS
the BIG TEXAN STEAK RANCH
NEW MEXICO
Lupton
Albuquerque
Tucumcari
Holbrook
Gallup
Blue Swallow MOTEL
422 MI.
Adrian
Amarillo
Shamrock
Catoosa
Tulsa
Luther
Arcadia
OKLAHOMA
959 MI.
TEXAS
Cadillac Ranch
BIG A
BIG A the Muffler Man

It was originally made of dirt like all the other roads, until one day it became the first fully paved all-weather highway.

No more getting stuck in the mud!

This led to more engines roaring. People road tripping.
Mom-and-pop shops opening.

People built filling stations.

They had dancing in fields
on weekends.

New people moved to Route 66 sharing their own traditions.

Farmers sold chickens and secret recipes.

Some people exchanged goods instead of money for a place to stay the night.

ALBERTA'S HOTEL
Welcome
ALBERTA'S SNACK SHACK
36
WORLD FAMOUS GLOBETROTTERS
HARLEM
GREEN BOOK 1954

Women opened businesses—alone.
This was uncommon at the time.

One guy even wrote a song about Route 66.
A famous singer named Nat King Cole sang it and made it popular!

Trading posts sold one-of-a-kind handmade goods.

Catchy ideas attracted big attention!

And quirky roadside attractions kept
popping up all along the road.

GEMINI GIANT   WILMINGTON, IL
Gemini Giant
1st MUFFLER MAN   FLAGSTAFF, AZ
TALL PAUL   "HOT DOG MUFFLER MAN"   ATLANTA, IL

Giant statues known as Muffler Men and Muffler Women
and a giant blue whale are popular ones.

Then Route 66, also known as The Mother Road, was replaced by a new highway.

There was less driving. It was barely surviving.

Some people moved away.

Some people stayed.

This led to minds thinking. Ideas flowing. People dreaming.

The first Historic Route 66 Association was formed to save
The Main Street of America.

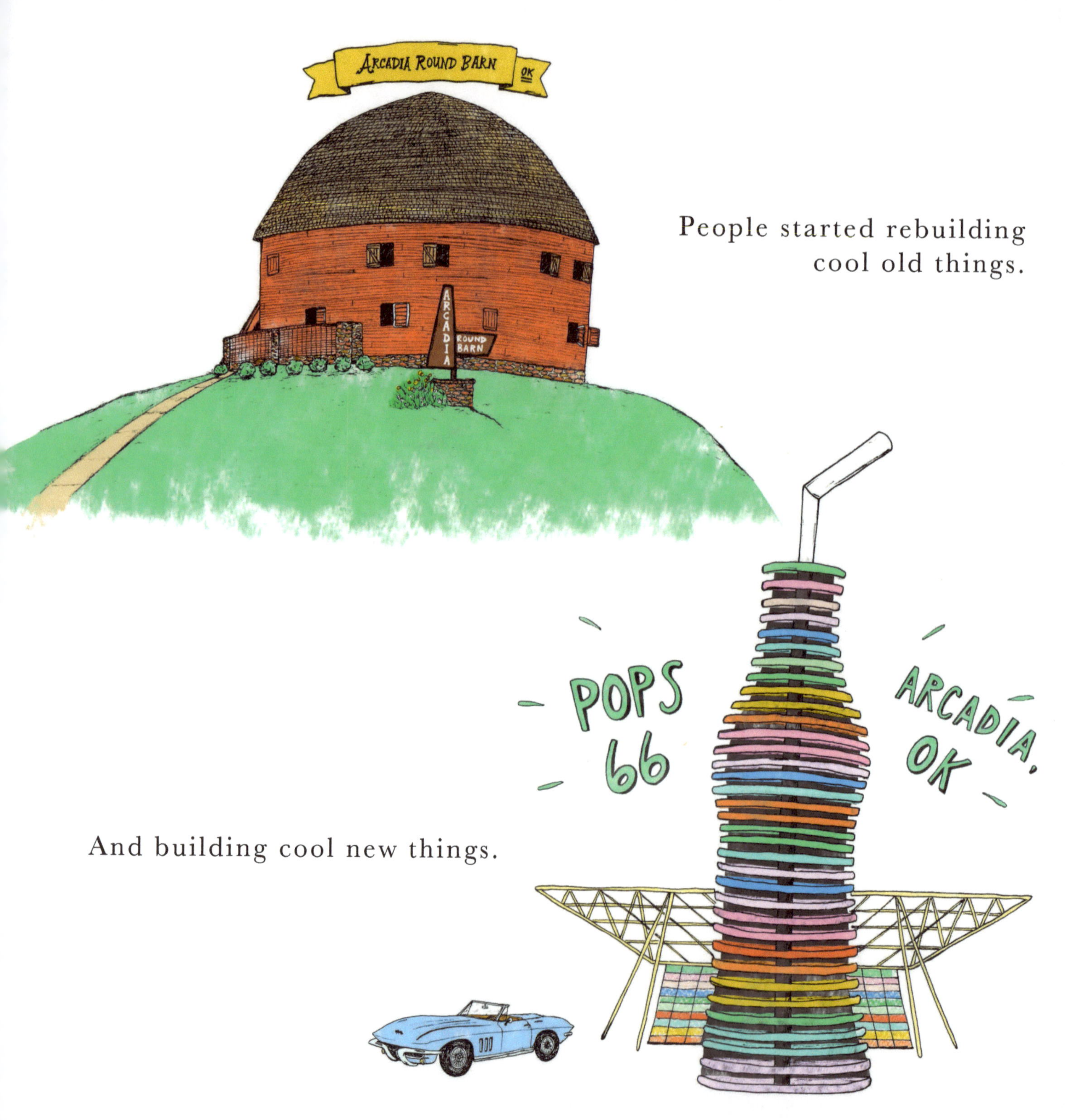

People started rebuilding
cool old things.

And building cool new things.

Today, Route 66 again has cars honking.
Neon buzzing. People busying.

And new kitschy roadside attractions that keep popping up.

At the heart of this iconic road and its revival are
people. The ones who built it and the ones who keep
it going!

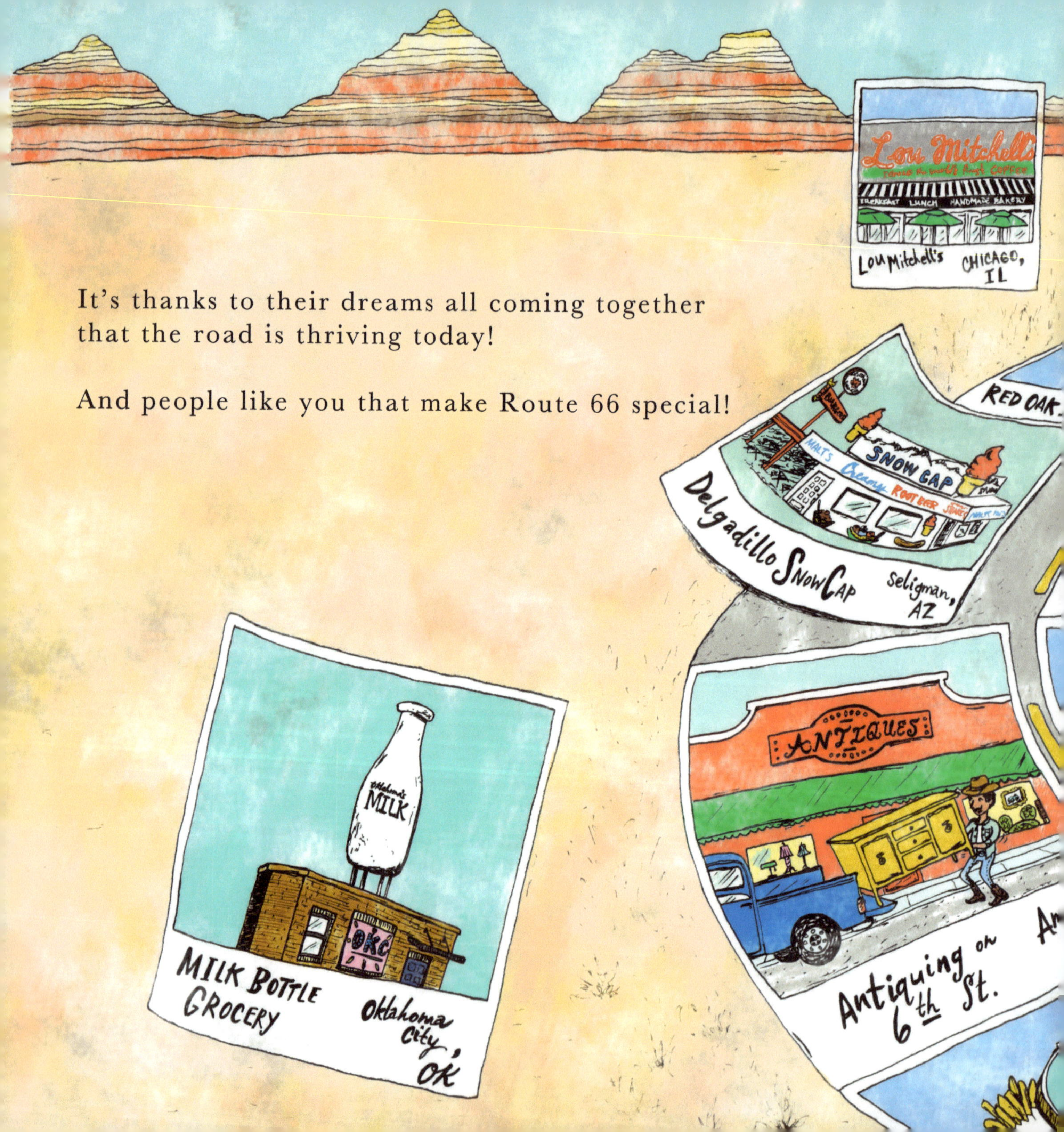

It's thanks to their dreams all coming together
that the road is thriving today!

And people like you that make Route 66 special!

HISTORIC
ROUTE
US
66
ROUTE
Painted Desert Inn
Petrified Forest National Park, AZ
LEANING TOWER of GROOM, TX
TEEPEE CURIOS TUCUMCARI, NM
ROUTE 66
COZY DOG DRIVE IN SPRINGFIELD, IL
MARKET FOOD ICE
RIVERTON STORE RIVERTON, KS
U DROP INN
GT 350
CRUISE
SIGN ON the Mother ROAD!
MIDPOINT CAFE
ADRIAN, TX
KINGMAN, AZ

PLACES ON ROUTE 66

Thanks to all the people that keep Route 66 going! Small, locally owned businesses are the heart of Route 66 and because of preservation and persistence, most of the stops in this book are still around today, plus many more.

ILLINOIS

Lou Mitchell's has been feeding hungry travelers since 1923. Don't miss out on the free donut holes for everyone! *565 W Jackson Blvd, Chicago, IL 60661* Historic Place

Dell Rhea's Chicken Basket started as a gas station lunch counter in the late 1930s. Legend has it that one day, two local farm women approached owner Irv Kolarik and promised to share a recipe for cooking fried chicken with him if he promised to buy their chickens and The Chicken Basket began. *645 Joliet Rd, Willowbrook, IL 60527* Historic Place

Cozy Dog Drive In claims the title of 'Home of the "Original" hot dog on a stick, dipped in batter and deep fried' and they've been serving them up since 1949 with the same recipe that Ed Waldmire developed in 1946. *2935 S 6th St, Springfield, IL 62703*

Pink Elephant Antique Mall has loads of antiques plus the retro Mother Road Fudge-n-Candy shop where you can eat fudge and candy made from vintage recipes, all inside the old Livingston High School building. Outside take some fun kitschy pictures with a giant pink elephant, muffler people, and more. *908 Veterans Memorial Dr, Livingston, IL 62058* PASSPORT STAMPS

Twistee Treat Diner is a 50s style diner with a giant ice cream cone building located at the Pink Elephant Antique Mall. *908 Veterans Memorial Dr, Livingston, IL 62058*

MISSOURI

Alberta's Hotel was opened in the 1940s by local entrepreneur Alberta Ellis serving all races. It was listed in the Green Book and several celebrities stayed here, including the Harlem Globetrotters. *625 N Benton Ave, Springfield, MO 65806* Demolished

Red Oak II was the brainchild of internationally known artist, Lowell Davis. It's part art installation and part neighborhood mixed with a blast from the past. It features buildings bought and moved from the original Red Oak to a farm. It's a private community that visitors can visit for free. *10917 County Loop 122, Carthage, MO 64836*

KANSAS

Big A Muffler Man is a newer muffler man located outside a restored Texico station at Gearhead Curios. *520 S Main St, Galena, KS 66739*

Old Riverton Store is a mom-and-pop shop and eatery that's remained nearly unchanged inside since it opened in 1925. Stop in and grab a sandwich, they get rave reviews! *7109 KS-66, Riverton, KS 66770* PASSPORT STAMPS & Historic Place

OKLAHOMA

Buck Atom's Cosmic Curios on 66 has a quirky selection of Route 66 goods located in a restored 1950s gas station. You can't miss it, just look for the 21-foot space cowboy Muffler Man, Buck Atom and his 19-foot space cowgirl companion, Stella Atom. You can even stay at Buck's Cosmic Crash Pad behind the shop! *1347 E 11th St, Tulsa, OK 74120* PASSPORT STAMPS

Blue Whale of Catoosa was completed in 1972 by Hugh S. Davis, a zoologist, for his wife and grandchildren. It's 20 feet tall and 80 feet long. Visit with a picnic basket for a memorable day of fishing and feeding the turtles with a giant blue whale! *2600 US Route 66, Catoosa, OK 74015*

Threatt Filling Station was the only known Black American-owned gas station and cafe on Route 66. The Threatt family built the filling station on the edge their farm in 1915 and rebuilt it in 1933. They also started an African American baseball team, had dances on the 150 acres of land, and were listed in the Green Book. It has been owned by the family for over 90 years and they spearheaded having it restored in 2023. *21940 OK-66, Luther, OK 73054* Historic Place

Arcadia Round Barn was built in 1898 by local farmer William Harrison Odor. He made it round because he thought it would be cyclone-proof according to his son. It was built without any straight walls by bending bur oak boards soaked while green and forced into the curves of the walls and rafters making it an engineering marvel.

Its restoration was completed in 1992 with the help of Luke Robison and a group of volunteers. *107 E Highway 66, Arcadia, OK 73007*

Pops 66 offers over 500 different sodas and beverages to try! Fill up with snacks and gas and check out the 66-foot neon pop bottle out front. *660 W Highway 66, Arcadia, OK 73007*

Milk Bottle Grocery is a giant milk bottle, on top of a tiny building, that was constructed in 1948 out of sheet metal. It's an example of quirky roadside marketing. *2426 North Classen Blvd, Oklahoma City, OK 73106*

TEXAS

Tower Station and U-Drop Inn Café is an Art Deco style building built in 1936 after a man named John Nunn drew his idea for it on the ground with an old nail. The U-Drop Inn Café got its name from a schoolboy's entry in a naming contest. *105 E 12th St, Shamrock, TX 79079*

Leaning Tower of Texas was installed by Ralph Britten in the early 1980s. After gaining attention on its side for two years, it was set upright and the CB conversations stopped. It was then reset at an angle for marketing. *I-40 US Rte 66, Groom, TX 79039*

Big Texan Steak Ranch opened in 1960 and is best known for owner R.J. Lee's marketing idea of the free 72 oz steak! Legend has it that after a contest where a cowboy ate 4 ½ pounds of steak (72 oz), plus all the fixings in one hour, Bob (R.J.) Lee stood up on a chair and proclaimed to everyone that from that day in 1962 forward, anyone who could eat it all in one hour would get it for FREE! *7701 I-40, Amarillo, TX 79118 (moved to new highway)*

6th Street is a 1-mile stretch of historic Route 66 filled with locally owned antique shops, record stores, book emporiums, eateries, and more! Stop by Texas Ivy Antiques to get your Route 66 passport stamped! *6th Street between Georgia and Western Streets, Amarillo, TX 79106*

Cadillac Ranch is a public art installation of 10 Cadillacs buried nose-down in the ground at the same angle as the pyramids of Giza. It was created by an art group called the Ant Farm in 1974. It's an interactive art piece, so you can spray paint them! It's even encouraged! *13651 I-40 Frontage Rd, Amarillo, TX 79124*

Midpoint Café is located at the midpoint of Route 66 where there's a sign to let you know you've reached it! They have lots of flavors of self-named "ugly pies" to choose from, like the Elvis with peanut butter, chocolate, and bananas! *305 Historic Route 66, Adrian, TX 79001*

NEW MEXICO

TeePee Curios started as a Gulf gas station in 1942. When Route 66 was widened in the late 1950s, early 60s, the gas pumps were removed and it became TeePee Curios. *924 E Route 66 Blvd, Tucumcari, NM 88401*

Blue Swallow Motel was an engagement gift in 1958 for 2nd owner Lillian Redman. She was dedicated to its longevity and reportedly said, "I end up traveling the highway in my heart with whoever stops here for the night." *815 E Route 66 Blvd, Tucumcari, NM 88401*

66 Diner transports you back to a retro dining experience straight out of the 1950s. They serve traditional diner fare with a soda fountain and a restored 1958 jukebox! It opened in 1987 in an old Phillips 66 gas station built in 1945. *1405 Central Ave NE, Albuquerque, NM 87106*

ARIZONA

Yellowhorse Trading Post was started by Juan "Chief" Yellowhorse, a Navajo Indian born in 1930. He opened his trading post as a place for Navajo people to sell their handmade goods. *I-40 Exit 359, Lupton, AZ 86508*

Painted Desert Inn was the vision of Herbert David Lore who built it around 1920 as a tourist attraction. Sadly, he built it on a seam of bentonite clay that began to cause cracks in the building. To save it, he sold it to the park in the 1930s "in order that it could be preserved and protected." *1 Park Rd, Petrified Forest National Park, AZ 86028*

Rainbow Rock Shop owner and artist Adam Luna spent 20 years building his assortment of concrete dinosaur statues. There's an impressive collection of geodes, stones, and petrified wood for sale too! *101 Navajo Blvd, Holbrook, AZ 86025*

Wigwam Motel was built by original owner Chester E. Lewis in 1950 after being inspired by the original Wigwam Village designed by Frank Redford in 1937. He purchased the rights to the name "Wigwam Village" with a unique royalty agreement where the dimes put in coin-operated radios in each wigwam went to Redford as payment. *811 W Hopi Dr, Holbrook, AZ 86025*

PASSPORT STAMPS

Jack Rabbit Trading Post is most recognizable by the clever marketing 'Here it is' sign and mile markers all along Route 66 showing the way to this trading post. It

all started when the original owner Jim Taylor moved to Joseph City, Arizona via convertible with a large black rabbit statue in the car in 1949! *3386 Historic U.S. 66, Joseph City, Arizona 86032*

Delgadillo's Snow Cap was built in 1953 by Juan Delgadillo (brother of Angel). The iconic outside has tons of fun things to look at and there's nothing more Route 66 than burgers, hot dogs, shakes and ice cream! *301 AZ-66, Seligman, AZ 86337*

Angel & Vilma Delgadillo's Original Route 66 Gift Shop started in Delgadillo's Barber Shop that he opened in the 1950s. Route 66 travelers helped fuel his dream to a reality with travelers stopping for haircuts until the new highway diverted traffic out of town and "the world forgot about us" according to Angel. He and Vilma started the gift shop and the first Historic Route 66 Association. *22265 Historic Route 66, Seligman, AZ 86337*

Mr. D'z Route 66 Diner is most famous for its colorful building, retro décor & root beer. *105 E. Andy Devine Ave, Kingman, AZ 86401*

CALIFORNIA

Mitla Café is famous for their hard-shell tacos! It was started by the Montaño family who wanted to serve traditional Mexican food after immigrating from Mexico in 1937 and it is still family owned and run in its original location. *602 N. Mount Vernon Ave, San Bernardino, CA 92411*

Santa Monica Pier Ferris Wheel was the first solar powered wheel in the world! It's since been updated with a newer version, but it still has the same iconic look with red and yellow gondolas! *380 Santa Monica Pier, Santa Monica, CA 90401*

OTHER MENTIONS IN THIS BOOK

(Get Your Kicks on) Route 66 was written by aspiring songwriter Bobby Troup. His wife Cynthia came up with the catchy Get Your Kicks on Route 66 line during a road trip across the country to Los Angeles in 1946. That same year, Nat King Cole recorded it and it became so popular, other singers wanted to sing it too.

Muffler Men and Women are giant statues of men and women. It all started in 1962 when a fiberglass artist named Bob Prewitt got an order for a 20-foot-tall Paul Bunyan statue. After months of working on the statue, the buyer never paid. So, Prewitt hit the road, Route 66, with his giant statue and sold it to the Lumberjack Café in Flagstaff, AZ. He then used the original mold to make many more!

For more places new & old on Route 66 visit HelloRoute66.com

Text © 2026 by Reese Traves • Illustrations © 2026 by Jon Traves • All rights reserved. No part of this book may be reproduced, transmitted, or stored in an information retrieval system in any form or by any means, graphic, electronic, or mechanical, including photocopying, taping, and recording, without prior written permission from the publisher. • First edition 2026 • Library of Congress Control Number: 2026910650 • ISBN 978-1-7346021-3-5 • 10 9 8 7 6 5 4 3 2 1 Printed in the United States of America • This book was typeset in Baskerville and the display type was hand-lettered by the illustrator • The illustrations were done in pen-and-ink and colored with digital magic • Published by Good Avenue Books • 2607 Wolflin Ave #145, Amarillo, TX 79109 • Visit us at www.goodave.com

To all the small, local business owners and people who love Route 66! - RT & JT

www.ingramcontent.com/pod-product-compliance
Lightning Source LLC
Chambersburg PA
CBHW042203030726
47602CB00007B/104